SIGN LANGUAGE LITERATURE SERIES

Ananse the Spider

Why Spiders Stay on the Ceiling

Illustrated by Kathy Kifer, Dahna Solar and Charla Barnard

Published by

Garlic Press
100 Hillview Lane #2
Eugene, OR 97408

ISBN 0-931993-85-7
Order Number GP-085

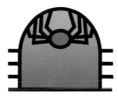

The **Sign Language Literature Series**
presents stories from different cultures. Ananse
the spider stories can be found from Africa to
the Caribbean. Ananse is a character who as
often shows his outlandishness as his princely
manner, his resourcefulness, or his greed.

This Ananse tale comes from the Ashanti
people of West Africa. It serves to tell why
spiders are found on ceilings. The story is
presented in simple language, full illustration,
and is complemented with illustrated signs.

Lion, King of animal, want know who most clever.

Lion, King of Beasts, wanted to know
who was the cleverest.

Ananse | brag

he | most | wise

and | clever.

Ananse the spider bragged that
he was the wisest and cleverest.

"You cannot fly," scolded the birds.

"I will show you," said Ananse.

Ananse gather many feather from forest many bird.

Ananse gathered many feathers
from the forest birds.

He · gather · rubber · from · rubber · tree · and · stick · many · feather · on · his · body.

He gathered rubber from the rubber tree
and stuck feathers all over his body.

Lion call every animal watch Ananse fly.

The Lion called every animal
to watch Ananse fly.

"Look, it is Ananse," they all shouted.

The eagle challenged Ananse
to follow him higher.

Sun

melt

rubber

hold

Ananse

many

feather

The sun melted the rubber
holding Ananse's many feathers.

Every animal, laugh

when Ananse fall.

Every animal laughed when Ananse fell.

Ananse fell on the soft palm branches of a house
and hurried into the roof.

Until now, that why spider stay on roof and ceiling so ashamed they.

To this day, that is why spiders stay on the roof
and ceiling, so ashamed are they.